WITHDRAWN

WELCOME TO THE U.S.A.
VIRGINIA

Written by Ann Heinrichs   Illustrated by Matt Kania
Content Adviser: William B. Obrochta, Director of Education,
Virginia Historical Society, Richmond, Virginia

The Child's World

Published in the United States of America by The Child's World®
PO Box 326 • Chanhassen, MN 55317-0326
800-599-READ • www.childsworld.com

Photo Credits

Cover: Photodisc; frontispiece: Brand X Pictures.

Interior: Blue Ridge Farm of Ferrum College: 22; Corbis: 6 (Jim Richardson), 14 (Dave G. Houser), 25 (Dave Bartruff), 29 (Charles E. Rotkin); Library of Congress: 16; Monticello/Thomas Jefferson Foundation: 30; Natural Bridge Wax Museum: 33; Richard T. Nowitz/Corbis: 21, 34; Photodisc: 26, 38; Virginia Department of Conservation and Recreation: 13; Virginia Tourism Corporation: 9, 10, 17 (Colonial Williamsburg Foundation), 18.

Acknowledgments

The Child's World®: Mary Berendes, Publishing Director

Editorial Directions, Inc.: E. Russell Primm, Editorial Director; Katie Marsico, Associate Editor; Judith Shiffer, Assistant Editor; Matt Messbarger, Editorial Assistant; Susan Hindman, Copy Editor; Melissa McDaniel, Proofreader; Kevin Cunningham, Peter Garnham, Matt Messbarger, Olivia Nellums, Chris Simms, Molly Symmonds, Katherine Trickle, Carl Stephen Wender, Fact Checkers; Tim Griffin/IndexServ, Indexer; Cian Loughlin O'Day, Photo Researcher and Editor

The Design Lab: Kathleen Petelinsek, Design; Julia Goozen, Art Production

Library of Congress Cataloging-in-Publication Data
Heinrichs, Ann.
  Virginia / by Ann Heinrichs ; cartography and illustrations by Matt Kania.
      p. cm. — (Welcome to the U.S.A.)
  Includes index.
  ISBN 1-59296-488-5 (library bound : alk. paper)
  1. Virginia—Juvenile literature. I. Kania, Matt, ill. II. Title.
  F226.3.H453 2006
  975.5—dc22   2005004813

Ann Heinrichs is the author of more than 100 books for children and young adults. She has also enjoyed successful careers as a children's book editor and an advertising copywriter. Ann grew up in Fort Smith, Arkansas, and lives in Chicago, Illinois.

About the Author
Ann Heinrichs

Matt Kania loves maps and, as a kid, dreamed of making them. In school he studied geography and cartography, and today he makes maps for a living. Matt's favorite thing about drawing maps is learning about the places they represent. Many of the maps he has created can be found in books, magazines, videos, Web sites, and public places.

About the
Map Illustrator
Matt Kania

On the cover: Ahoy! Jamestown settlers used ships like these almost 400 years ago!
On page one: Don't forget to check out scenic Shenandoah National Park!

OUR VIRGINIA TRIP

Let's take a tour through Virginia! There's so much you can explore there.

You'll build sand castles. You'll watch wild ponies swimming. You'll visit a wigmaker and meet Thomas Jefferson. You'll hang out with soldiers from the 1700s. You'll do farm chores and see great inventions. And you'll gaze at massive rock formations.

Just follow that loopy dotted line. Or just skip around. Either way, you're in for a great ride. Now hop aboard and buckle up. We're on our way through Virginia!

WELCOME TO VIRGINIA

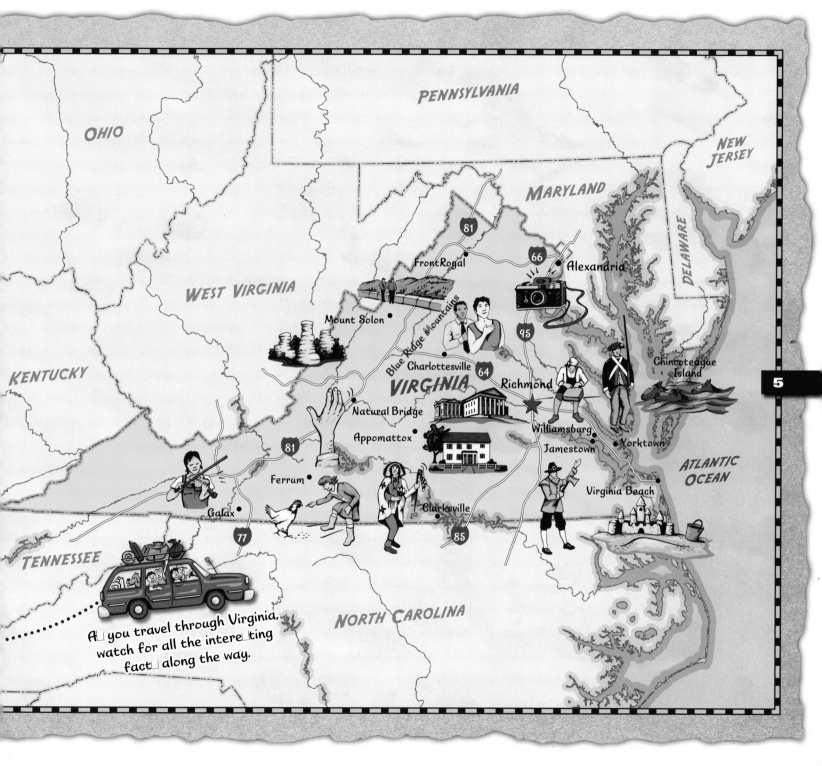

As you travel through Virginia, watch for all the interesting facts along the way.

Visitors take in the scenic Blue Ridge Mountains.

What a view! You're winding down Skyline Drive. It runs along the top of the Blue Ridge Mountains. You pass ragged cliffs and forested mountainsides. Far below is the beautiful Shenandoah Valley.

Western Virginia lies within the Appalachian Mountain range. The Blue Ridge Mountains are in this range. The Piedmont Region covers central Virginia. It has many hills and rolling plains.

Eastern Virginia is called the Tidewater Region. Virginia has a long, ragged coastline. It faces Chesapeake Bay and the Atlantic Ocean. Across Chesapeake Bay is the Delmarva **Peninsula.**

The Great Dismal Swamp is southwest of Norfolk. It's Virginia's largest wetland.

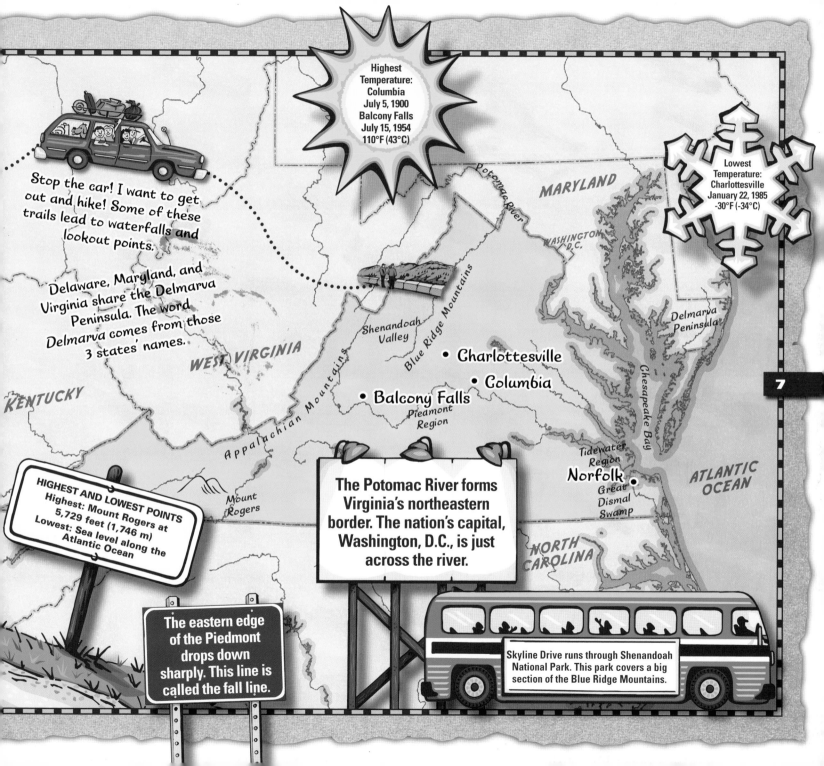

Highest Temperature:
Columbia
July 5, 1900
Balcony Falls
July 15, 1954
110°F (43°C)

Lowest Temperature:
Charlottesville
January 22, 1985
-30°F (-34°C)

Stop the car! I want to get out and hike! Some of these trails lead to waterfalls and lookout points.

Delaware, Maryland, and Virginia share the Delmarva Peninsula. The word Delmarva comes from those 3 states' names.

MARYLAND

WASHINGTON, D.C.

Potomac River

Delmarva Peninsula

KENTUCKY

WEST VIRGINIA

Appalachian Mountains

Shenandoah Valley

Blue Ridge Mountains

Piedmont Region

• Charlottesville

• Columbia

• Balcony Falls

Chesapeake Bay

Tidewater Region

Norfolk

Great Dismal Swamp

ATLANTIC OCEAN

Mount Rogers

HIGHEST AND LOWEST POINTS
Highest: Mount Rogers at 5,729 feet (1,746 m)
Lowest: Sea level along the Atlantic Ocean

The Potomac River forms Virginia's northeastern border. The nation's capital, Washington, D.C., is just across the river.

NORTH CAROLINA

The eastern edge of the Piedmont drops down sharply. This line is called the fall line.

Skyline Drive runs through Shenandoah National Park. This park covers a big section of the Blue Ridge Mountains.

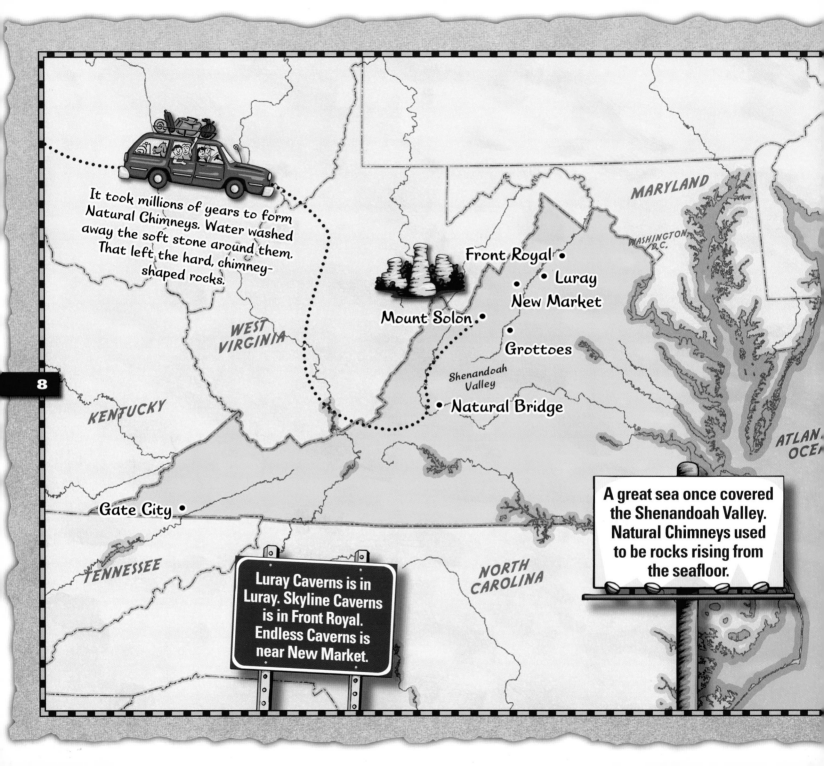

It took millions of years to form Natural Chimneys. Water washed away the soft stone around them. That left the hard, chimney-shaped rocks.

MARYLAND

WASHINGTON D.C.

Front Royal •
• Luray
New Market

Grottoes

Mount Solon •

Shenandoah Valley

• Natural Bridge

WEST VIRGINIA

KENTUCKY

Gate City •

TENNESSEE

NORTH CAROLINA

ATLANTIC OCEAN

A great sea once covered the Shenandoah Valley. Natural Chimneys used to be rocks rising from the seafloor.

Luray Caverns is in Luray. Skyline Caverns is in Front Royal. Endless Caverns is near New Market.

Chimneys, Tunnels, and Caves

Do they look like giant chimneys? Or castle towers? Visit Natural Chimneys and see what *you* think. These rock towers are awesome!

Natural Chimneys is near Mount Solon. It's one of Virginia's many natural wonders. Another is Natural Tunnel, near Gate City. A creek cut this tunnel through the mountains. Natural Bridge, near the town of Natural Bridge, is a huge rock arch.

Underground streams created Virginia's many caverns, or caves. You'll find several caverns in the Shenandoah Valley. One is Grand Caverns, near Grottoes. Others include Luray, Skyline, and Endless caverns.

Meet you on the other side! Don't forget to check out Natural Tunnel.

Historic Garden Week is in April. Many big homes and gardens across Virginia are open to visitors then.

Splash! Crowds gather to watch the Chincoteague Wild Pony Swim.

The 1st Chincoteague Wild Pony Swim took place in 1925.

The Chincoteague Wild Pony Swim

Splash! The wild ponies jump into the water. They churn up the water as they swim. At last, they climb ashore.

These frisky ponies live on Assateague Island. Once a year, the ponies are rounded up. Then they swim across to Chincoteague Island. There they are sold. This keeps a limit on the pony population.

Many animals live in Virginia's forests. They include deer, beavers, bobcats, foxes, and raccoons. Black bears live in the mountains.

The coastal wetlands are home to ducks and geese. Crabs, oysters, and clams live along Chesapeake Bay. Whales and dolphins swim in the Atlantic Ocean.

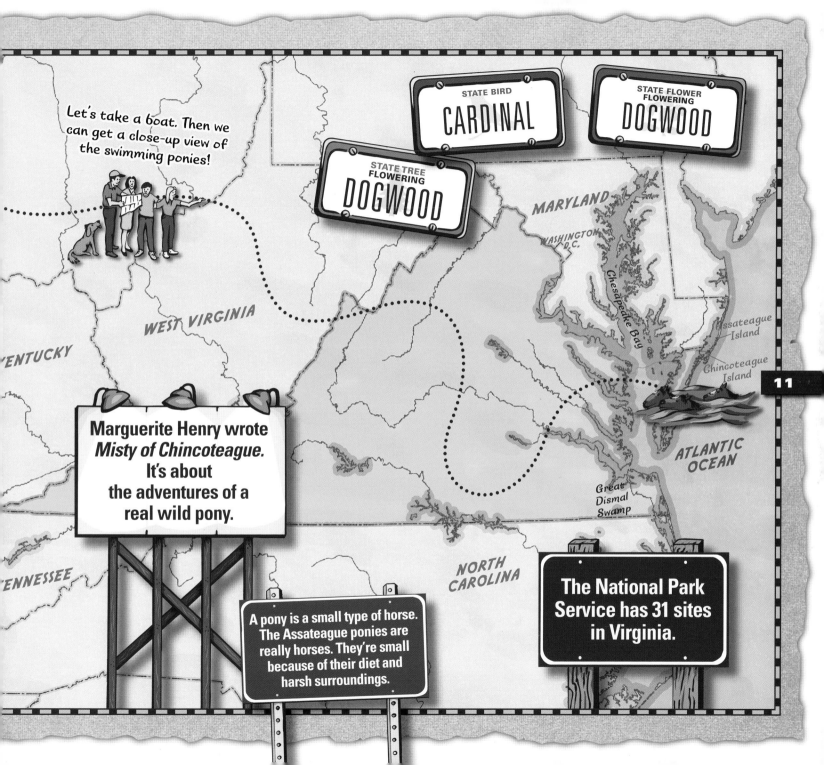

Let's take a boat. Then we can get a close-up view of the swimming ponies!

STATE TREE
FLOWERING
DOGWOOD

STATE BIRD
CARDINAL

STATE FLOWER
FLOWERING
DOGWOOD

MARYLAND

WASHINGTON, D.C.

Chesapeake Bay

WEST VIRGINIA

KENTUCKY

Assateague Island

Chincoteague Island

ATLANTIC OCEAN

Marguerite Henry wrote *Misty of Chincoteague*. It's about the adventures of a real wild pony.

Great Dismal Swamp

TENNESSEE

NORTH CAROLINA

A pony is a small type of horse. The Assateague ponies are really horses. They're small because of their diet and harsh surroundings.

The National Park Service has 31 sites in Virginia.

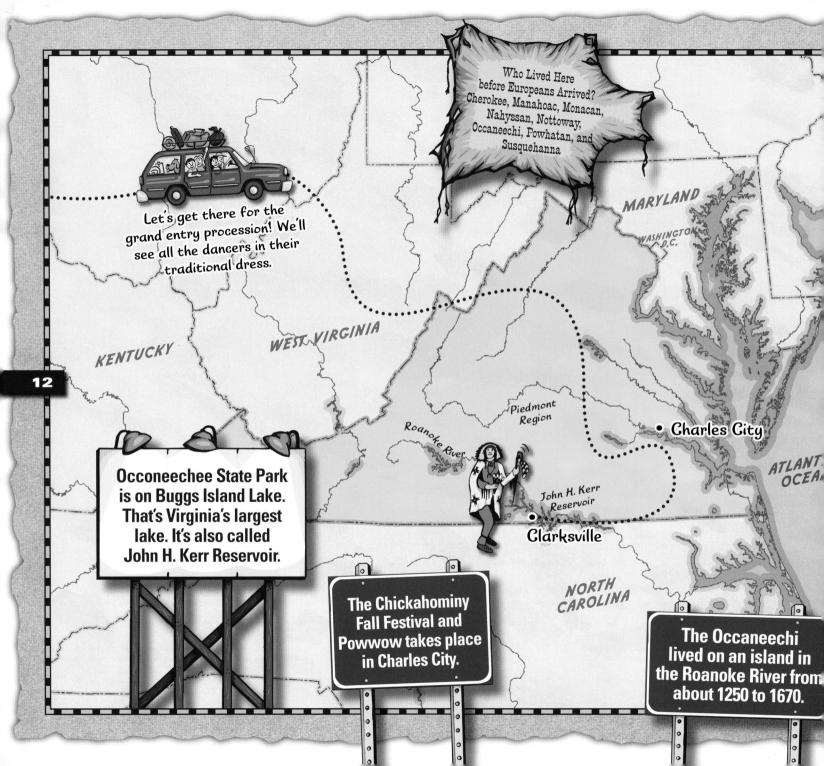

Who Lived Here before Europeans Arrived? Cherokee, Manahoac, Monacan, Nahyssan, Nottoway, Occaneechi, Powhatan, and Susquehanna

Let's get there for the grand entry procession! We'll see all the dancers in their traditional dress.

MARYLAND

WASHINGTON D.C.

KENTUCKY

WEST VIRGINIA

Piedmont Region

Roanoke River

Charles City

John H. Kerr Reservoir

ATLANTIC OCEAN

Clarksville

Occoneechee State Park is on Buggs Island Lake. That's Virginia's largest lake. It's also called John H. Kerr Reservoir.

NORTH CAROLINA

The Chickahominy Fall Festival and Powwow takes place in Charles City.

The Occaneechi lived on an island in the Roanoke River from about 1250 to 1670.

The Native American Heritage Festival and Powwow

Dancers in feathers and fringe stomp and swirl around. The drummers keep up a steady beat. Meanwhile, delicious smells drift from the food stands.

You're attending the Native American Heritage Festival and Powwow. It takes place near Clarksville's Occoneechee State Park. This park is named for a Native American group.

Virginia was once home to many Indians. They spoke Algonquian, Siouan, and Iroquoian languages. Some lived along the coast. They caught fish and gathered shellfish. Others lived in the hilly Piedmont Region.

The Occaneechi lived in the Piedmont. They settled on an island in the Roanoke River.

A Native American dancer performs at Occoneechee State Park.

Jamestown Settlement

Ahoy! This historical interpreter works at the Jamestown Settlement. He speaks from aboard a ship there.

Climb aboard a sailing ship. Then watch blacksmiths and carpenters at work. You're exploring Jamestown Settlement!

English settlers arrived nearby in 1607. They set up the Virginia **Colony.** In time, there would be thirteen English colonies. Jamestown was the colonies' first permanent settlement.

Thousands of **colonists** settled near the coast. They raised tobacco and other crops. Many farmers owned plantations, or huge farms. African American slaves did the farmwork. New settlers moved farther west in the colony. They sometimes clashed with Indian groups.

Virginia formed its own colonial government. Most leaders were wealthy farmers.

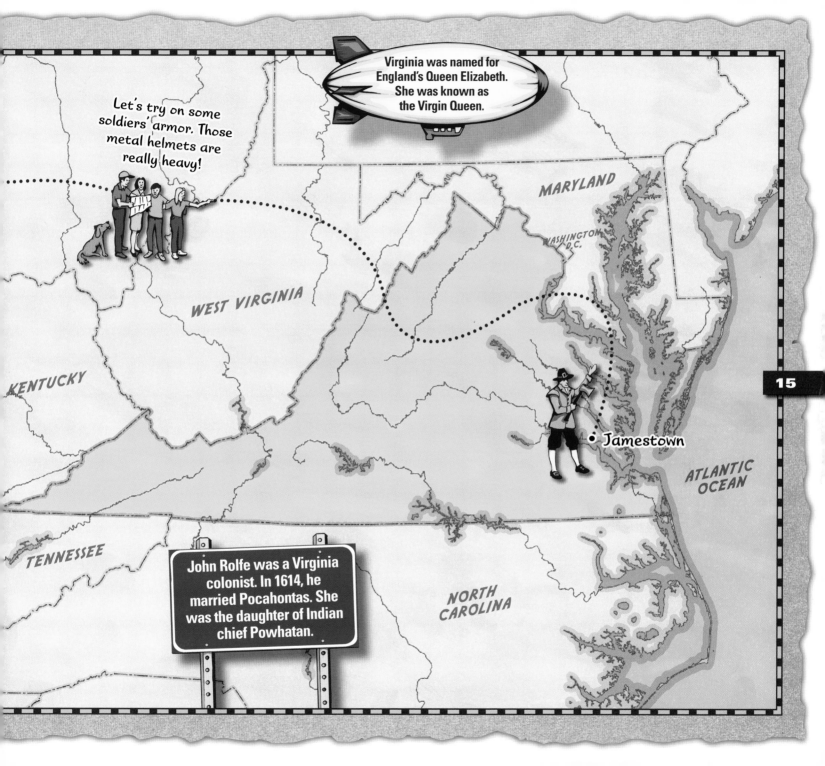

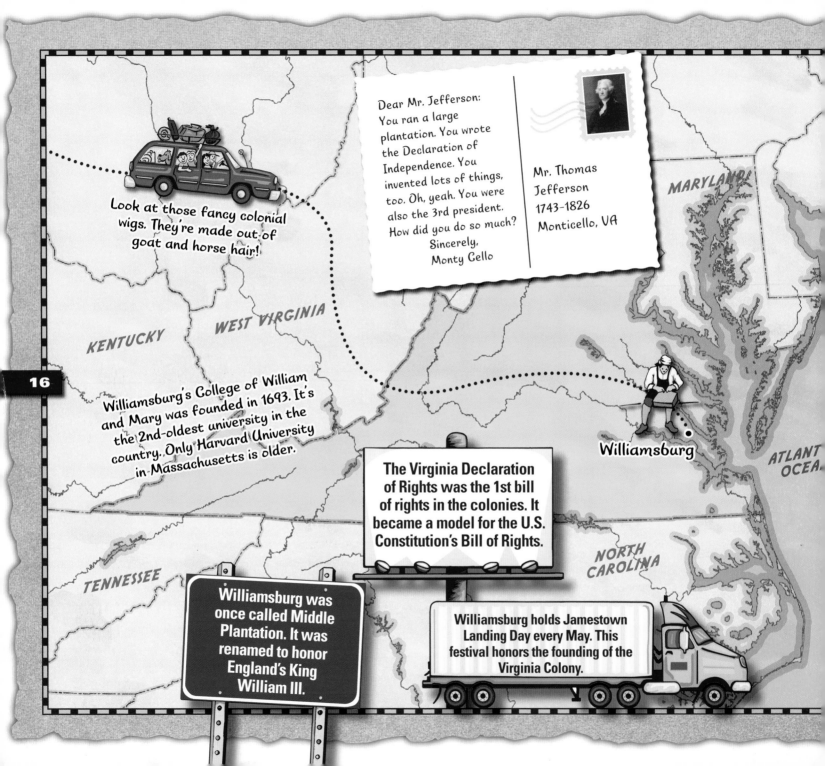

Look at those fancy colonial wigs. They're made out of goat and horse hair!

Dear Mr. Jefferson:
You ran a large plantation. You wrote the Declaration of Independence. You invented lots of things, too. Oh, yeah. You were also the 3rd president. How did you do so much?
Sincerely,
Monty Cello

Mr. Thomas Jefferson
1743-1826
Monticello, VA

MARYLAND

KENTUCKY

WEST VIRGINIA

Williamsburg's College of William and Mary was founded in 1693. It's the 2nd-oldest university in the country. Only Harvard University in Massachusetts is older.

Williamsburg

ATLANT OCEA.

The Virginia Declaration of Rights was the 1st bill of rights in the colonies. It became a model for the U.S. Constitution's Bill of Rights.

NORTH CAROLINA

TENNESSEE

Williamsburg was once called Middle Plantation. It was renamed to honor England's King William III.

Williamsburg holds Jamestown Landing Day every May. This festival honors the founding of the Virginia Colony.

Colonial Williamsburg

The shoemaker sews leather by hand. The **apothecary** offers cures for aches and pains. The print shop prints colonial newspapers. Other merchants make fancy hats and wigs. You're back in the 1700s at Colonial Williamsburg!

Williamsburg was a bustling city in colonial times. It became Virginia's capital in 1699. Colonial leaders made many important decisions there. They passed the Virginia Declaration of Rights in 1776. It promised basic freedoms to all citizens.

Virginia's General Court held sessions in Williamsburg, too. Plantations owners came from miles around to attend. They did business with the many local merchants.

Craftsmen are hard at work in Colonial Williamsburg.

Williamsburg was Virginia's capital from 1699 to 1780.

Strike up a tune! Musicians play at the Old Fiddler's Convention.

Clogging and flatfoot dancing are traditional Appalachian dance styles.

The Old Fiddler's Convention in Galax

Check out the Old Fiddler's Convention in Galax. You'll see and hear a lot more than fiddling! There are folk singers and flatfoot dancers. Some people play fiddles, banjos, and guitars. Others play instruments you may never have seen before. These include autoharps, mandolins, dobros, and dulcimers.

Folk music and dancing are old Virginia **traditions.** They are folk arts of the Appalachian Region. Settlers came there from England, Scotland, and Ireland. They brought their music and dances with them. Over time, these arts took on new qualities. People even added African American and Indian features. Today, music lovers are keeping these traditions alive.

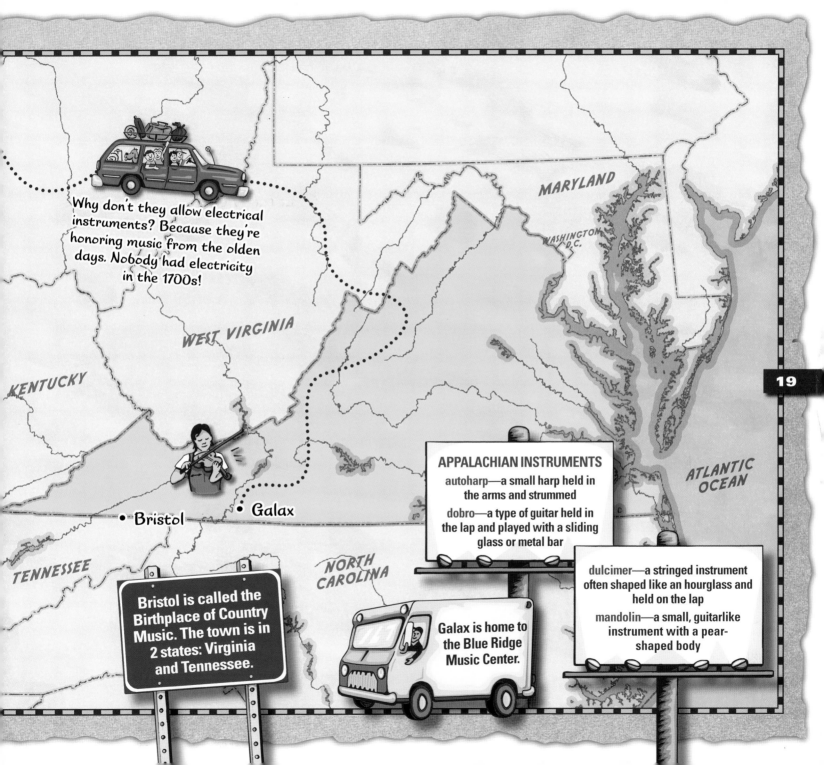

MARYLAND

WASHINGTON D.C.

WEST VIRGINIA

KENTUCKY

Why don't they allow electrical instruments? Because they're honoring music from the olden days. Nobody had electricity in the 1700s!

ATLANTIC OCEAN

• Bristol   • Galax

TENNESSEE

NORTH CAROLINA

APPALACHIAN INSTRUMENTS

autoharp—a small harp held in the arms and strummed

dobro—a type of guitar held in the lap and played with a sliding glass or metal bar

dulcimer—a stringed instrument often shaped like an hourglass and held on the lap

mandolin—a small, guitarlike instrument with a pear-shaped body

Bristol is called the Birthplace of Country Music. The town is in 2 states: Virginia and Tennessee.

Galax is home to the Blue Ridge Music Center.

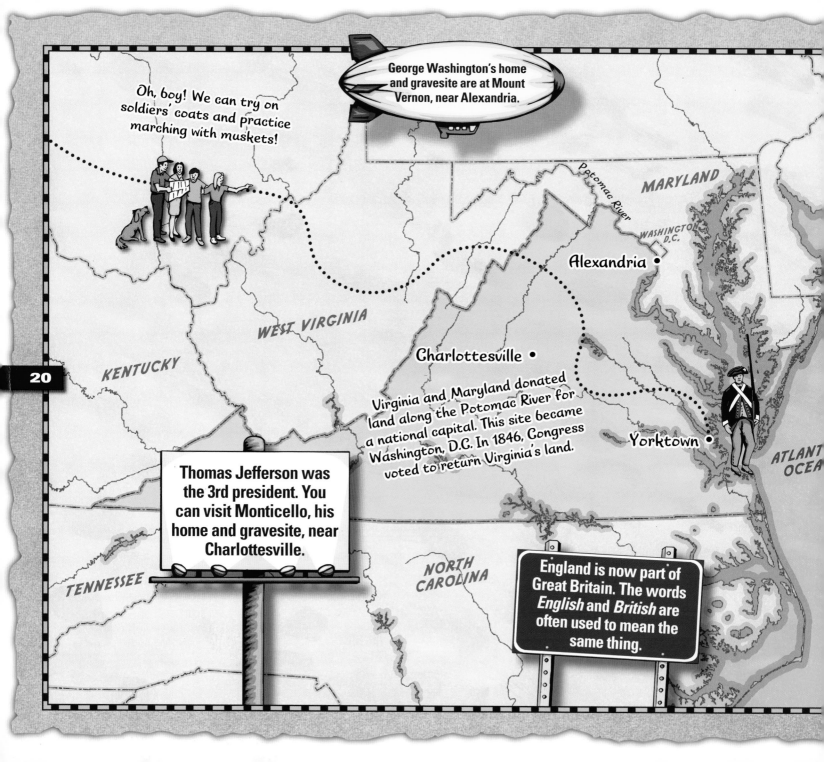

Yorktown and the Revolutionary War

How did colonial soldiers live? How did their guns work? How did they get the food they needed? Just stop by Yorktown Victory Center. Costumed guides show you all about soldiers' lives.

Yorktown was an important place in colonial history. The colonists wanted freedom from Great Britain. They fought the Revolutionary War (1775–1783). General George Washington led the colonial army.

Many battles were fought in Virginia. The final battle took place at Yorktown. Britain's Lord Cornwallis surrendered there in 1781. Then the colonies became the United States of America. General Washington became the first president.

Salute! The Yorktown Victory Center features performers in colonial costumes.

Virginia was the 10th state to enter the Union. It joined on June 25, 1788.

Chincoteague Island holds an oyster festival every October.

Driving oxen sure is hard work! Find out for yourself at Blue Ridge Farm.

Apples are an important crop in the Shenandoah Valley.

Blue Ridge Farm in Ferrum

Blue Ridge Farm is a great place to visit. It's just like a farm in 1800. Costumed workers are doing their daily chores. They're baking bread or tending the farm animals. You can even help with some of these activities.

Almost everyone in Virginia used to farm. Farming is a smaller industry now. Today, many farmers raise chickens and beef cattle. These animals are the leading farm products. Growing tobacco was once Virginia's major industry. Tobacco is still the top crop today.

Fishing is a big industry in Virginia. Fishers haul in tons of oysters and crabs. They catch lots of fish, too!

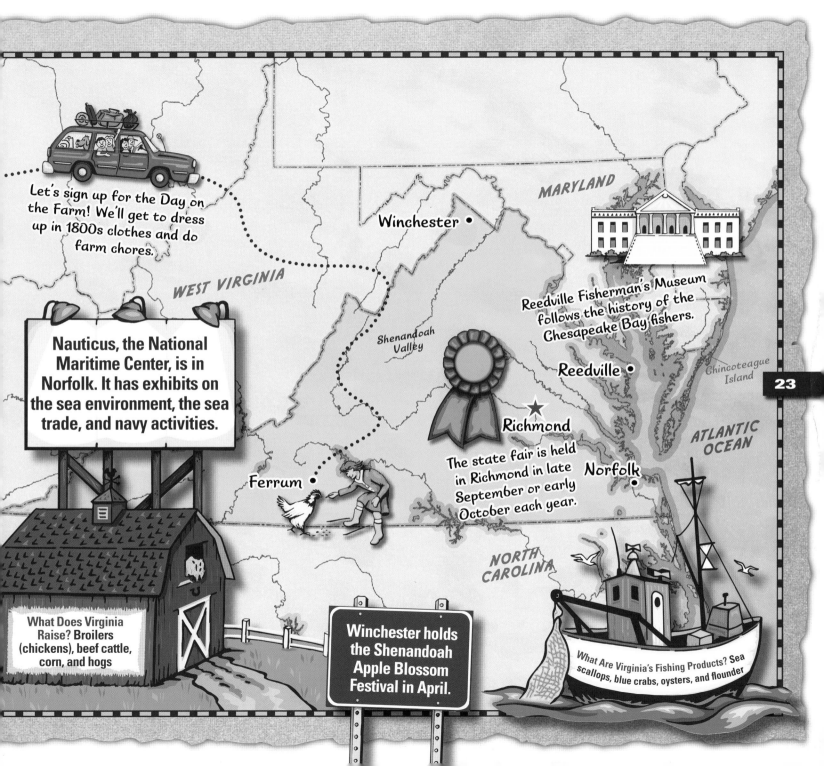

Let's sign up for the Day on the Farm! We'll get to dress up in 1800s clothes and do farm chores.

MARYLAND

Winchester •

WEST VIRGINIA

Shenandoah Valley

Reedville Fisherman's Museum follows the history of the Chesapeake Bay fishers.

Reedville •

Chincoteague Island

Nauticus, the National Maritime Center, is in Norfolk. It has exhibits on the sea environment, the sea trade, and navy activities.

Richmond ★

The state fair is held in Richmond in late September or early October each year.

ATLANTIC OCEAN

Norfolk •

Ferrum •

NORTH CAROLINA

What Does Virginia Raise? Broilers (chickens), beef cattle, corn, and hogs

Winchester holds the Shenandoah Apple Blossom Festival in April.

What Are Virginia's Fishing Products? Sea scallops, blue crabs, oysters, and flounder

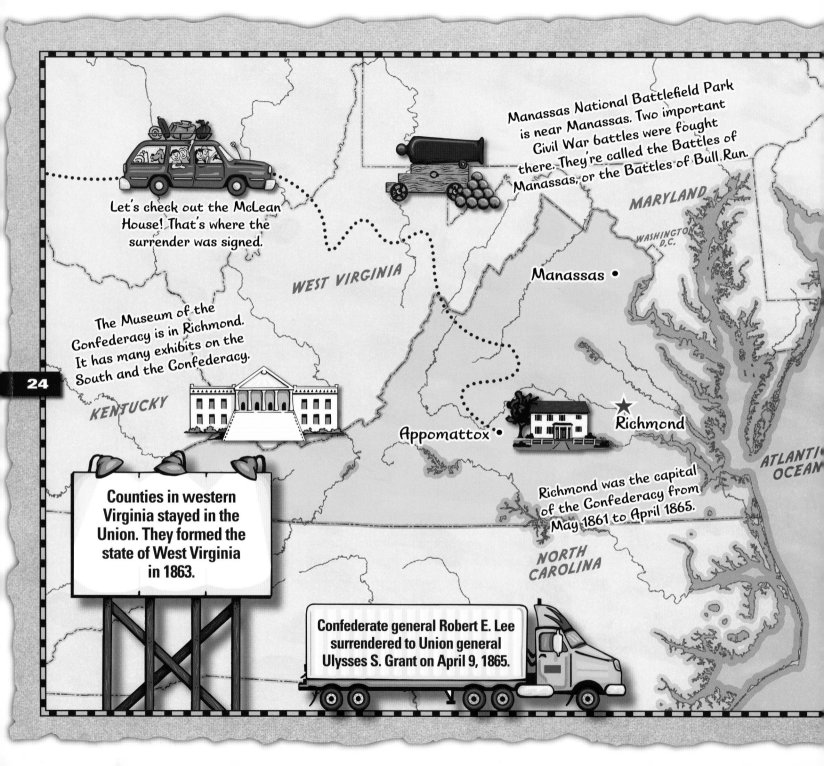

Manassas National Battlefield Park is near Manassas. Two important Civil War battles were fought there. They're called the Battles of Manassas, or the Battles of Bull Run.

MARYLAND

WASHINGTON D.C.

Let's check out the McLean House! That's where the surrender was signed.

WEST VIRGINIA

Manassas •

The Museum of the Confederacy is in Richmond. It has many exhibits on the South and the Confederacy.

KENTUCKY

Appomattox •

★ Richmond

ATLANTIC OCEAN

Counties in western Virginia stayed in the Union. They formed the state of West Virginia in 1863.

Richmond was the capital of the Confederacy from May 1861 to April 1865.

NORTH CAROLINA

Confederate general Robert E. Lee surrendered to Union general Ulysses S. Grant on April 9, 1865.

Appomattox Court House and the Civil War

Virginia was the site of 123 Civil War battles.

Learn to set up a camp. Go through military **drills** with a soldier. Hear some **rousing** music from the 1860s. You're taking part in Children's Civil War Day!

This event takes place at Appomattox Court House. The court house is now part of a historical park. It's an important Civil War (1861–1865) site. The states fought this war over slavery.

Northern states formed the Union side. They wanted to outlaw slavery. Southern states made up the Confederacy. Confederate states wanted to keep slavery. Virginia joined the Confederate side. In the end, the Union forces won. The surrender was signed at Appomattox Court House.

Important decisions were made in this room. You're touring General Grant's headquarters at Appomattox.

Confederate generals Robert E. Lee, Stonewall Jackson, and Jeb Stuart were Virginians.

25

Virginia lawmakers are busy inside the capitol in Richmond.

26

Do you know what all the presidents looked like? You can test yourself on eight of them. Their statues are in the state capitol. Why are they there? All eight were born in Virginia!

The capitol is the center of state government. Inside are many state government offices. Virginia's government has three branches. One branch makes the state's laws. It's called the General Assembly. Another branch carries out the laws. The governor heads this branch. The third branch is made up of judges. They decide whether laws have been broken.

Virginia's official name is the Commonwealth of Virginia. Three other states are called commonwealths: Kentucky, Massachusetts, and Pennsylvania.

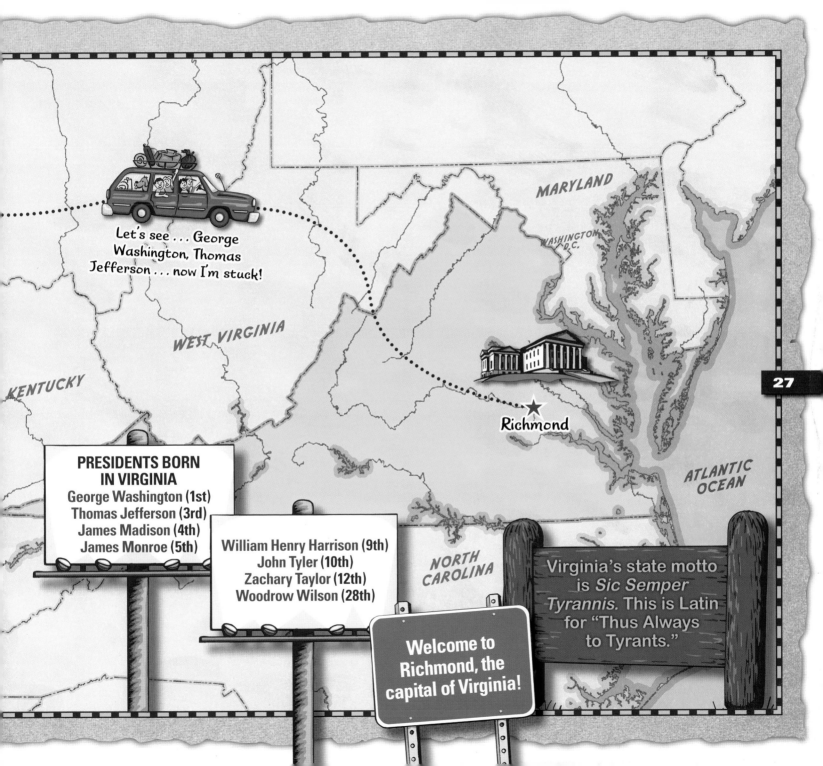

Let's see ... George Washington, Thomas Jefferson ... now I'm stuck!

MARYLAND

WASHINGTON, D.C.

WEST VIRGINIA

KENTUCKY

Richmond

ATLANTIC OCEAN

PRESIDENTS BORN IN VIRGINIA
George Washington (1st)
Thomas Jefferson (3rd)
James Madison (4th)
James Monroe (5th)

William Henry Harrison (9th)
John Tyler (10th)
Zachary Taylor (12th)
Woodrow Wilson (28th)

NORTH CAROLINA

Welcome to Richmond, the capital of Virginia!

Virginia's state motto is *Sic Semper Tyrannis.* This is Latin for "Thus Always to Tyrants."

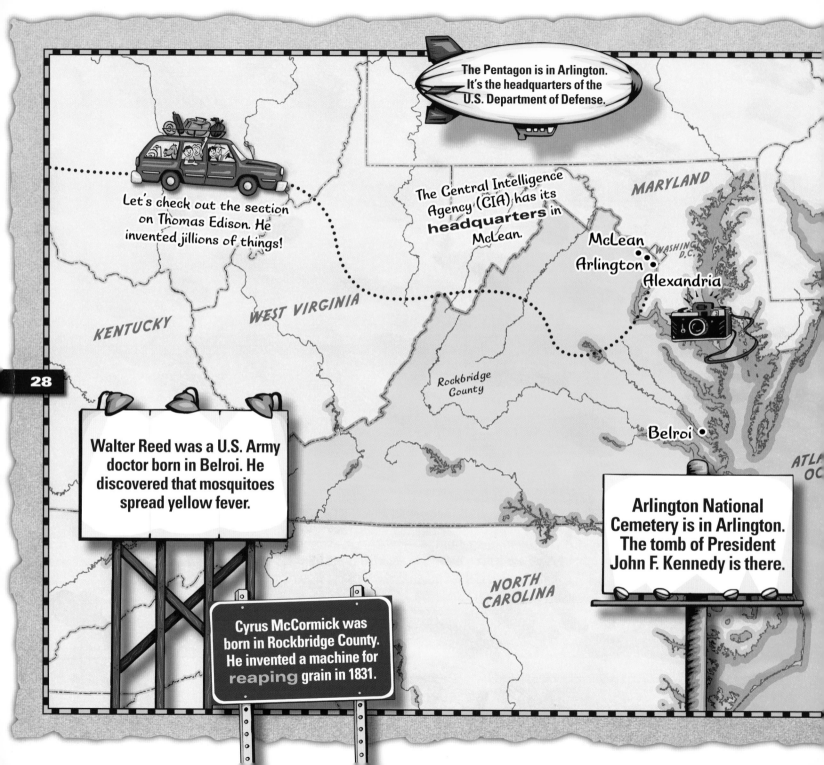

The Pentagon is in Arlington. It's the headquarters of the U.S. Department of Defense.

The Central Intelligence Agency (CIA) has its **headquarters** in McLean.

MARYLAND

Let's check out the section on Thomas Edison. He invented jillions of things!

McLean

Arlington

WASHINGTON D.C.

Alexandria

KENTUCKY

WEST VIRGINIA

Rockbridge County

Belroi

Walter Reed was a U.S. Army doctor born in Belroi. He discovered that mosquitoes spread yellow fever.

ATLANTIC OCEAN

Arlington National Cemetery is in Arlington. The tomb of President John F. Kennedy is there.

NORTH CAROLINA

Cyrus McCormick was born in Rockbridge County. He invented a machine for **reaping** grain in 1831.

The U.S. Patent and Trademark Museum in Alexandria

Think about bicycles, toys, and cameras. Someone invented each one. Inventors must get a **patent** or **trademark.** These help prevent copying.

Want to learn all about inventions? Just visit the U.S. Patent and Trademark Museum.

Inventions helped Virginia's **industries** grow. In the 1880s, Virginia was making many products. These included cigarettes, cotton cloth, and ships.

By the mid-1900s, Washington, D.C., was filling up. So many U.S. government offices were opened in Virginia. One is the U.S. Patent and Trademark Office.

A man works with cloth at a Virginia textile mill.

About 1 out of 5 Virginians is African American.

New citizens recite the Pledge of Allegiance at Monticello.

The process by which a foreign citizen becomes a U.S. citizen is called naturalization.

Becoming Citizens at Monticello

The place is Monticello, Thomas Jefferson's home. The day is the Fourth of July. People from Europe, Asia, and Africa are here. Today, they become citizens of the United States.

This ceremony takes place every year. It's a big moment for those who attend.

Virginia has always welcomed **immigrants**. Early settlers came from England, Ireland, and Germany. Later, people came from all over the world. Today, Virginians have roots in many lands. Thousands of Filipinos live around Norfolk. People of many **cultures** live in northern Virginia. They include Vietnamese, **Hispanic,** and Korean people.

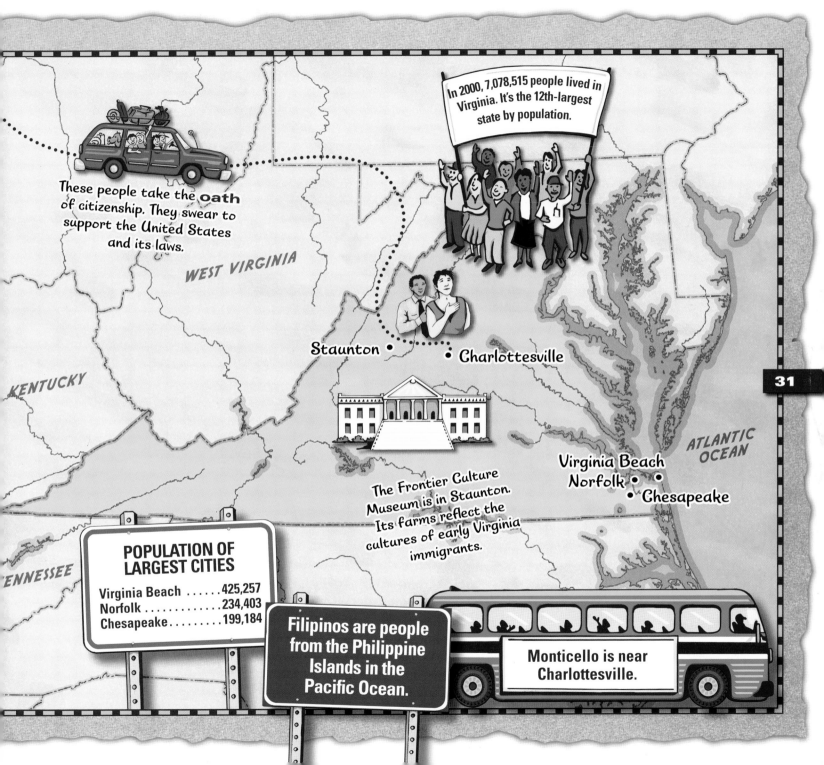

These people take the **oath** of citizenship. They swear to support the United States and its laws.

In 2000, 7,078,515 people lived in Virginia. It's the 12th-largest state by population.

WEST VIRGINIA

KENTUCKY

Staunton •

• Charlottesville

The Frontier Culture Museum is in Staunton. Its farms reflect the cultures of early Virginia immigrants.

ATLANTIC OCEAN

Virginia Beach
Norfolk • •
 • Chesapeake

TENNESSEE

POPULATION OF LARGEST CITIES

Virginia Beach 425,257
Norfolk 234,403
Chesapeake 199,184

Filipinos are people from the Philippine Islands in the Pacific Ocean.

Monticello is near Charlottesville.

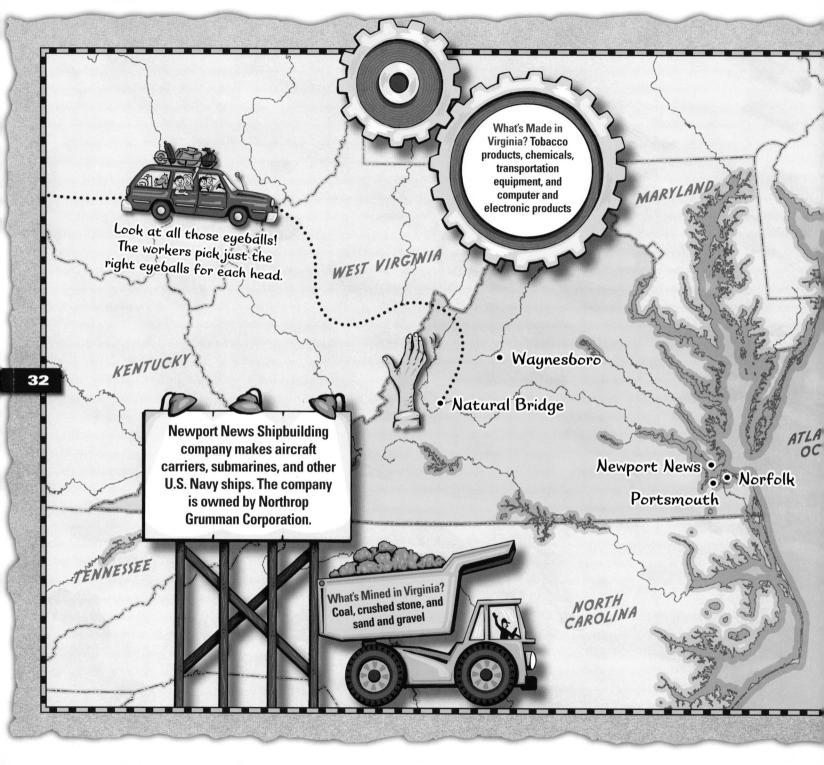

Look at all those eyeballs! The workers pick just the right eyeballs for each head.

What's Made in Virginia? Tobacco products, chemicals, transportation equipment, and computer and electronic products

Newport News Shipbuilding company makes aircraft carriers, submarines, and other U.S. Navy ships. The company is owned by Northrop Grumman Corporation.

What's Mined in Virginia? Coal, crushed stone, and sand and gravel

MARYLAND

WEST VIRGINIA

KENTUCKY

Waynesboro

Natural Bridge

Newport News

Norfolk

Portsmouth

ATLA OC

TENNESSEE

NORTH CAROLINA

Making Wax Figures in Natural Bridge

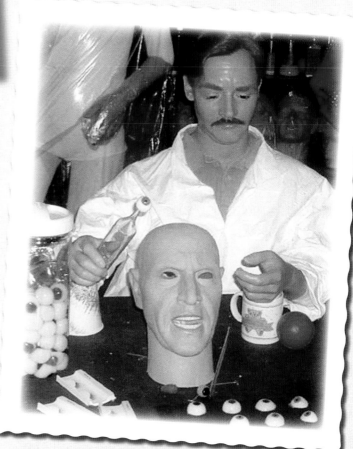

Yikes! Is it Halloween? Nope, just a day at the Wax Museum in Natural Bridge.

Here are some arms. There's a head. Body parts are everywhere. But they're not real. They're wax! Workers put them all together. They make wax figures of famous people.

You're visiting the Wax Museum in Natural Bridge. It has a really unusual factory. But Virginia has lots of normal factories, too.

Tobacco products are the leading factory goods. Soft drinks are important products, as well. Many factories make medicines. Others make nylon and rayon fibers.

Virginia also makes boats and big ships. Newport News, Norfolk, and Portsmouth are shipbuilding cities.

Virginia Metalcrafters is in Waynesboro. It makes metal goods such as lamps, garden statues, and fireplace tools. You can watch the workers pour and shape the melted metal.

Pass the suntan lotion! Enjoy a trip to Virginia Beach.

People even come from foreign countries to compete in the sand sculpting contest!

Building Sand Castles in Virginia Beach

Are you good at building sand castles? Then enter the North American Sand Sculpting Championship! It's part of Virginia Beach's Neptune Festival. People come with buckets and shovels. Some bring wheelbarrows, ladders, and garden tools! They build amazing things out of sand.

Virginia Beach is a popular vacation spot. People enjoy many activities along the coast. They go swimming, boating, or fishing. They even take whale-watching tours.

Some people head for Virginia's rugged mountains. They hike, watch wildlife, or explore caves. Others visit museums and historic sites. Whatever you enjoy, you'll find it in Virginia!

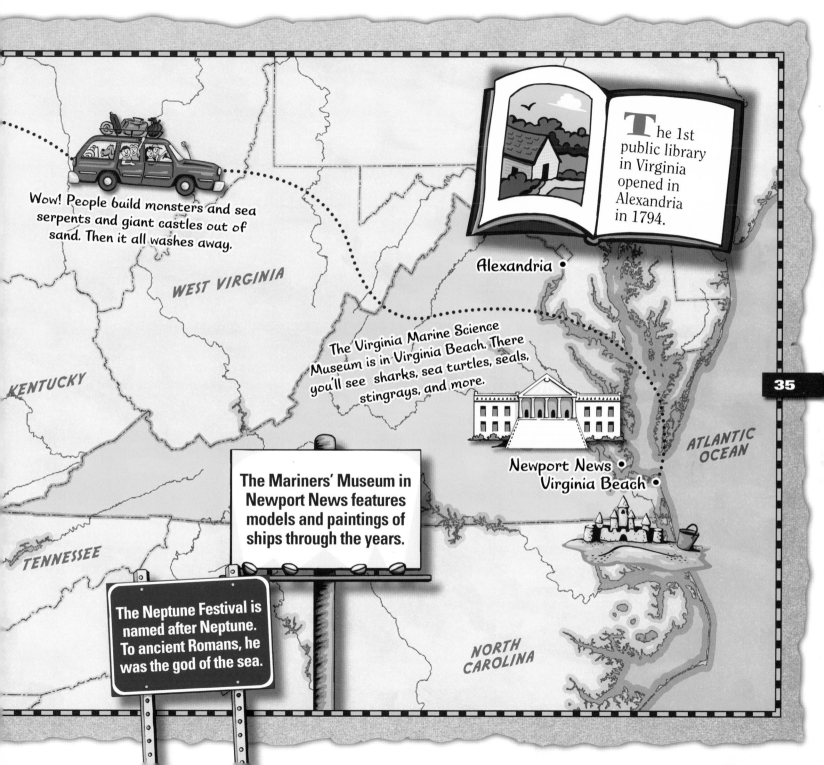

Wow! People build monsters and sea serpents and giant castles out of sand. Then it all washes away.

The 1st public library in Virginia opened in Alexandria in 1794.

WEST VIRGINIA

Alexandria •

KENTUCKY

The Virginia Marine Science Museum is in Virginia Beach. There you'll see sharks, sea turtles, seals, stingrays, and more.

ATLANTIC OCEAN

The Mariners' Museum in Newport News features models and paintings of ships through the years.

Newport News •
Virginia Beach •

TENNESSEE

The Neptune Festival is named after Neptune. To ancient Romans, he was the god of the sea.

NORTH CAROLINA

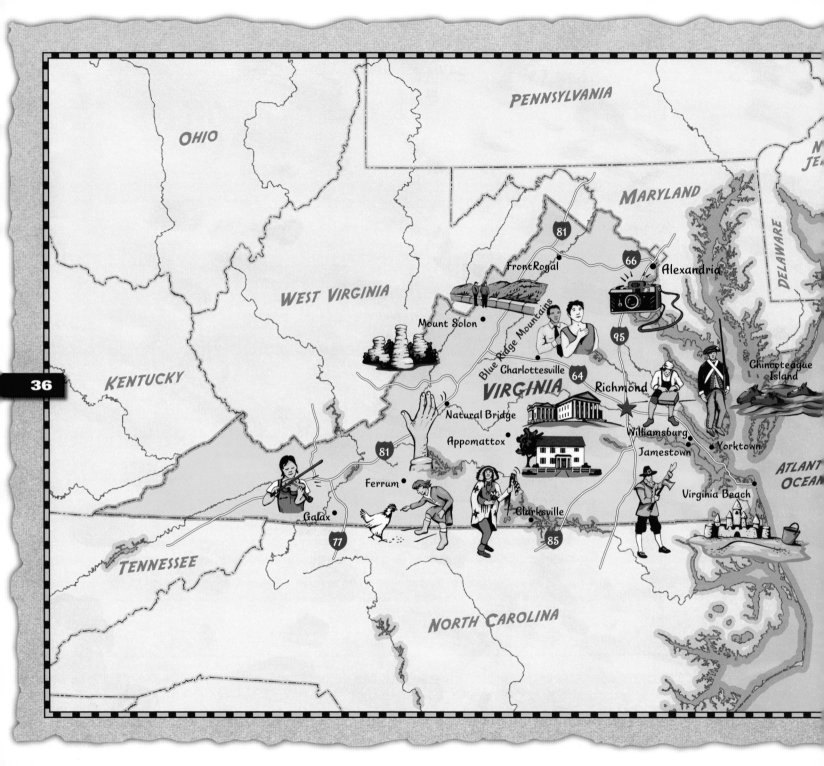

PENNSYLVANIA

OHIO

MARYLAND

WEST VIRGINIA

81

FrontRoyal

66

Alexandria

Mount Solon

Blue Ridge Mountains

95

Charlottesville

DELAWARE

N JE

KENTUCKY

VIRGINIA

64

Richmond

Chincoteague
Island

Natural Bridge

Williamsburg

Appomattox

Jamestown

Yorktown

81

ATLANT
OCEAN

Ferrum

Virginia Beach

77

Galax

Clarksville

85

TENNESSEE

NORTH CAROLINA

OUR TRIP

We visited many amazing places on our trip! We also met a lot of interesting people along the way. Look at the map on the left. Use your finger to trace all the places we have been.

When did the 1st Chincoteague Wild Pony Swim take place? See page 10 for the answer.

Where is the Chickahominy Fall Festival and Powwow held? Page 12 has the answer.

Who did Pocahontas marry? See page 15 for the answer.

When was Williamsburg Virginia's capital? Look on page 17 for the answer.

What are some typical Appalachian dancing styles? Page 18 has the answer.

What city is called the Birthplace of Country Music? Turn to page 19 for the answer.

Where is George Washington's gravesite located? Look on page 20 to find out!

Where is President John F. Kennedy buried? Turn to page 28 for the answer.

That was a great trip! We have traveled all over Virginia!
There are a few places that we didn't have time for, though. Next time, we plan to visit Thomas Jefferson's Poplar Forest near Bedford. This was his retreat home. Jefferson traveled to Lynchburg to escape the crowds who gathered at Monticello. Archeologists and architects are working to fully restore the house and land.

More Places to Visit in Virginia

WORDS TO KNOW

apothecary (uh-PO-thuh-kair-ee) an early type of drugstore; also, the druggist working there

colonists (KOL-uh-nists) people who settle a new land for their home country

colony (KOL-uh-nee) a land settled and governed by another country

cultures (KUHL-churz) the customs, beliefs, and ways of life of various groups of people

drills (DRILZ) military exercises

headquarters (HED-kwor-turz) the home office of an organization

Hispanic (hiss-PAN-ik) having roots in Spanish-speaking lands

immigrants (IM-uh-gruhnts) people who move into another country

industries (IN-duh-streez) types of business

oath (OHTH) a solemn promise

patent (PAT-uhnt) the legal right to make and sell an invention

peninsula (puh-NIN-suh-luh) a piece of land almost completely surrounded by water

reaping (REEP-ing) cutting grain at harvest

rousing (ROUZ-ing) something that is interesting or exciting

trademark (TRADE-mark) words or symbols indicating the company that legally owns a product

traditions (truh-DISH-uhnz) customs passed down for many years

Virginia covers 39,594 square miles (102,548 sq km). It's the 37th-largest state in size.

STATE SYMBOLS

State beverage: Milk

State bird: Cardinal

State boat: Chesapeake Bay deadrise

State dog: American foxhound

State fish: Brook trout

State flower: Flowering dogwood

State folk dance: Square dance

State fossil: *Chesapecten jeffersonius*

State insect: Tiger swallowtail butterfly

State shell: Oyster shell

State tree: Flowering dogwood

State flag

State seal

STATE SONG

Virginia has no state song. "Carry Me Back to Old Virginia" was once the state song. In 1997, the state legislature voted to remove it. In 1998, the legislature sponsored a contest to find a new state song. A winner has not yet been chosen.

FAMOUS PEOPLE

Ashe, Arthur (1943–1993), tennis champion

Beatty, Warren (1937–), actor and director

Clark, William (1770–1838), explorer

Cline, Patsy (1932–1963), country music singer

Fitzgerald, Ella (1917–1996), jazz singer

Henry, Patrick (1736–1799), patriot during the American Revolution

Jefferson, Thomas (1743–1826), 3rd U.S. president

Lee, Robert E. (1807–1870), commander of the Confederate army

Lewis, Meriwether (1774–1809), explorer

Madison, James (1751–1836), 4th U.S. president

Mourning, Alonzo (1970–), basketball player

Paterson, Katherine (1932–), children's author

Pocahontas (ca. 1595–1617), American Indian who helped the English settlers

Rylant, Cynthia (1954–), children's author

Scott, Winfield (1786–1866), hero of the Mexican War

Turner, Nat (1800–1831), preacher and slave

Washington, Booker T. (1856–1915), educator and founder of Tuskegee Institute

Washington, George (1732–1799), 1st U.S. president

Wilson, Woodrow (1856–1924), 28th U.S. president

Wolfe, Tom (1931–), author and journalist

Woodson, Carter (1875–1950), historian

TO FIND OUT MORE

At the Library

Adler, David A., and Ronald Himler (illustrator). *A Picture Book of Lewis and Clark.* New York: Holiday House, 2003.

Dexter, Robin, and R. W. Alley (illustrator). *Young Arthur Ashe: Brave Champion.* Mahwah, N.J.: Troll Associates, 1996.

Edwards, Pamela Duncan, and Troy Howell (illustrator). *O Is for Old Dominion: A Virginia Alphabet.* Chelsea, Mich.: Sleeping Bear Press, 2004.

Heinrichs, Ann. *Patrick Henry: Orator and Patriot.* Chanhassen, Minn.: The Child's World, 2004.

Pinkney, Andrea David, Scat Cat Monroe, and Brian Pinkney (illustrator). *Ella Fitzgerald: The Tale of a Vocal Virtuosa.* New York: Jump at the Sun/Hyperion Books for Children, 2002.

On the Web

Visit our home page for lots of links about Virginia:
http://www.childsworld.com/links

Note to Parents, Teachers, and Librarians: We routinely verify our Web links to make sure they are safe, active sites—so encourage your readers to check them out!

Places to Visit or Contact

Virginia Historical Society
428 North Boulevard
Richmond, VA 23220
804/358-4901
For more information about the history of Virginia

Virginia Tourism Corporation
901 East Byrd Street
Richmond, VA 23219
804/786-2051
For more information about traveling in Virginia

INDEX

Bye, Old Dominion State. We had a great time. We'll come back soon!